IN DREAMS

ORACLE GUIDEBOOK

by Boris Indrikov

10 9 8 7 6 5 4 3 2 1

Made in China

Translation from Russian
by Anna Kouprianova

Published by
U.S. GAMES SYSTEMS, INC.
179 Ludlow Street
Stamford, CT 06902 USA
www.usgamesinc.com

INTRODUCTION TO THE IN DREAMS ORACLE DECK

Since ancient times, humans have tried to see into the future. They looked into the smoke of the burning fire and tried to predict future events. They peered closely into patterns on a turtle's shell to find some answers. They glanced up into the night sky full of stars and tried to predict the future by watching the movement of the planets. With time, fortune-telling techniques got more and more complicated. First, it was colorful stones that one would toss up in the air. Later, there were small animal bones to help to solve the mystery of the future, which eventually became a complicated system of hexagrams, developed in China, as well as the mighty Book of Changes (I Ching). As the history of humankind unfolds, playing cards found their way from India into Europe and America and a new fortune-telling method emerged based on card readings. With time and knowledge those card reading techniques gave birth to a more complicated, grandiose and very deep and insightful system called tarot. Nowadays, people can learn to predict the future and try to unveil their own fortunes.

I find all this very interesting and fascinating. I have spent many years studying astrology and the great Chinese Book of Changes. On many occasions tarot cards stopped my heart with delight upon an accurate prediction. Once I published some of my paintings as a set of postcards and later I found out that some people use them as metaphorical maps and utilize them during psychotherapy sessions. Then and there I decided that I would develop my own unique divination system. I wanted to make it accessible and simple, because the more complex the set, the more likely that the sacred meanings would be lost in elaborate predictions.

There are 41 cards in the *In Dreams Oracle* deck. The 40 main cards are divided into four groups specified by different colors just like playing cards, which have four distinguished suits. Each group corresponds to a specific natural element and a certain sphere of human life.

Blue........... AIR............ external events
Red............ FIRE .... action
Green........ WATER..... feelings, emotions
Yellow....... EARTH..... material world

The cards are also divided into 10 categories that represent interaction of human and the outer world.

The 41st card is a prototype of the Joker. It does not belong to any of the suits. The days when you pull this card are very special days. On a day that Joker comes into your life it is advised that you and the world just observe each other.

HOW TO USE
IN DREAMS ORACLE CARDS

Find a quiet spot where you won't be disturbed. Concentrate. Take the cards into your left hand. Become one with the deck, imagine that the cards are the continuation of you, mentally connect with the set. Open your mind. Don't expect a "yes" or "no" answer to your question; it's not as simple as that. It's more like asking for direction. Keep in mind a situation in your life that you would like to resolve and ask "which way shall I move?" With your right hand pull out a single card from the deck and put it in front of you. Ultimately, divination with one card is the most effective approach. Your single card will give you the best answer and you won't be confused by all the different meanings and combinations of ideas in multiple cards. It doesn't matter if the card is upside down. If we browse through a book of art prints we recognize images either way. If we come across Mona Lisa by Leonardo da Vinci we'd still see Mona Lisa even if we look at the painting upside down.

Read the message on the card. Pay attention to what category and what natural element this card belongs to. Take in the message, thinking carefully about it. Use your imagination and intuition to interpret the advice given. Keep in mind that in this life there are no unsolvable problems. There are no bad or good people; there is only our reaction to what is happening in our lives in a given moment in time. Always remember: there is no good without evil and there is no light without darkness.

On one hand, faith is predetermined, which means nothing is an accident. On the other hand life is full of surprises, which means it is completely unpredictable.

So, you find yourself in the unique situation: between randomness of choosing a card and the certainty of its prediction when it falls into your hand.

Enjoy your communication with *In Dreams Oracle!*

THE CARDS

1
PLAY
AIR • EXTERNAL EVENTS

A message will change your life.

It is not the strongest of the species
that survives, nor the most intelligent,
but the one most responsive to change.

— CHARLES DARWIN —

2
PLAY
FIRE • ACTION

Let go of your biases.

If you let your past go, it doesn't mean that your past will let you go.

3
PLAY

WATER • FEELINGS • EMOTIONS

Welcome new feelings
and emotions.
Try something new.

True love is rare, and it's the only thing that gives life real meaning.

— NICHOLAS SPARKS —
(FROM *MESSAGE IN A BOTTLE*)

4
PLAY
EARTH • MATERIAL WORLD

A new beneficial offer
brings unexpected gain.

May the most you wish for
be the least you get.
(IRISH TOAST)

5
LOOK FOR HARMONY AND BALANCE

AIR • EXTERNAL EVENTS

All trouble passes away
and the world shines
with its true colors.

Fall seven times and stand up eight.
(JAPANESE PROVERB)

6
LOOK FOR HARMONY AND BALANCE

FIRE • ACTION

Resolve a conflict
and come to an agreement.

Always forgive your enemies.
Nothing annoys them more.

— OSCAR WILDE —

7
LOOK FOR HARMONY AND BALANCE

WATER • FEELINGS • EMOTIONS

Resolve inner conflict.

If you want to be somebody
—somebody really special—
be yourself!

8

LOOK FOR HARMONY AND BALANCE

EARTH • MATERIAL WORLD

Confidence returns,
life gains order, and
balance is restored.

Your life is not a problem to be solved,
but a gift to be opened.

— WAYNE MULLER —

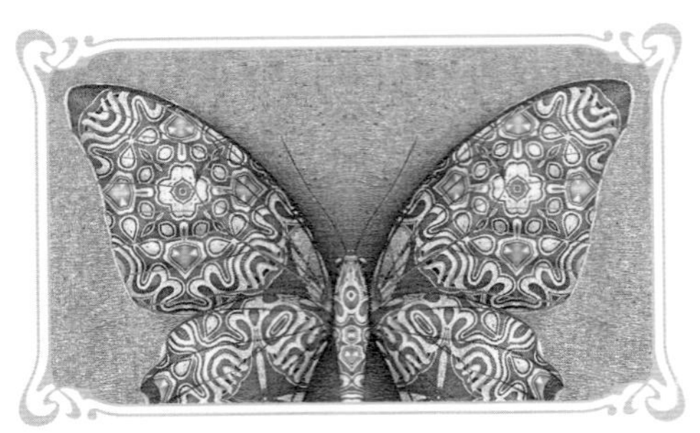

9
RENEW

AIR • EXTERNAL EVENTS

A new beginning
is just around the corner.
Get ready for a change.

Those who would like to be
constant in happiness and wisdom
must change often.

— CONFUCIUS —

10
RENEW

FIRE • ACTION

Destroy your patterns.
Act unexpectedly.
Change your situation.

Twenty years from now, you'll be more disappointed by the things that you didn't do than by the ones you did do.

— MARK TWAIN —

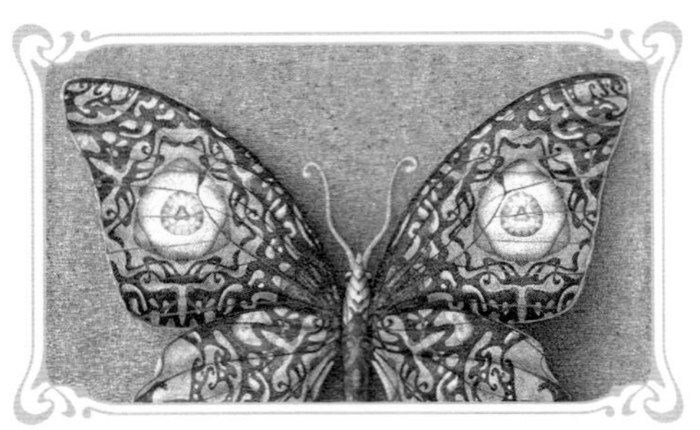

11
RENEW

WATER • FEELINGS • EMOTIONS

Look at the world with new perception.

The two most important days in your life are the day you are born and the day you find out why.

— MARK TWAIN —

12
RENEW
EARTH • MATERIAL WORLD

You want change,
renew your wardrobe.

Failure does not mean I don't have the talent; It means I have to try it in a different way.

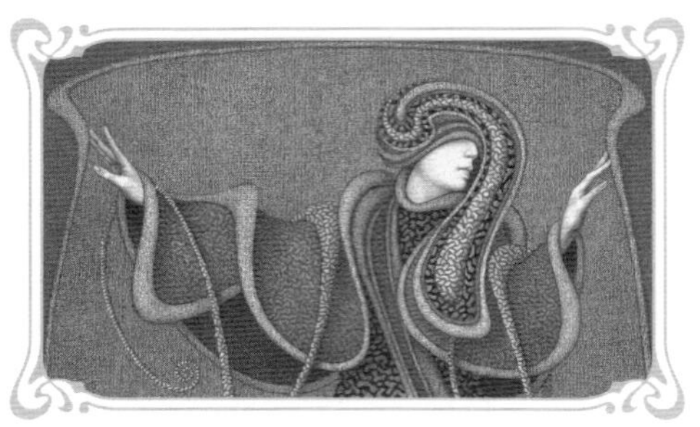

13
STOP AND GET TO KNOW YOURSELF

AIR • EXTERNAL EVENTS

Forthcoming events will make you change your internal perspectives.

To be yourself in a world that is constantly trying to make you something else is the greatest accomplishment.

— RALPH WALDO EMERSON —

14
STOP AND GET TO KNOW YOURSELF

FIRE • ACTION

Keep calm and start your internal change today.

Life is 10% what happens to me and 90% of how I react to it.

— CHARLES SWINDOLL —

15
STOP AND GET TO KNOW YOURSELF

WATER • FEELINGS • EMOTIONS

Look for the harmony within.

When we see men of worth, we should think of being like them; when we see men of a contrary character, we should turn inwards and examine ourselves.

— CONFUCIUS —

16
STOP AND GET TO KNOW YOURSELF

EARTH • MATERIAL WORLD

Stay home. Read a favorite book.
Remember happy moments.

Life is not about finding yourself.
Life is about creating yourself.

— LOLLY DASKAL —

17
LOVE TO INTERACT

AIR • EXTERNAL EVENTS

You might meet your soulmate.

You know you're in love when you can't fall asleep because reality is finally better than your dreams.

— DR. SEUSS —

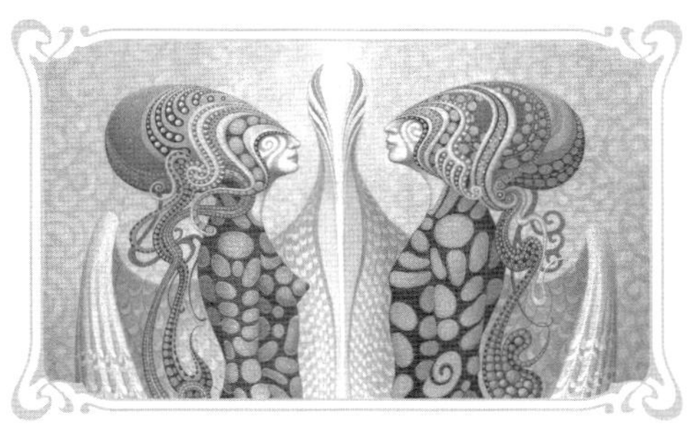

18
LOVE TO INTERACT
FIRE • ACTION

Help thy neighbor.

You yourself, as much as anybody in the entire universe, deserve your love and affection.

— BUDDHA —

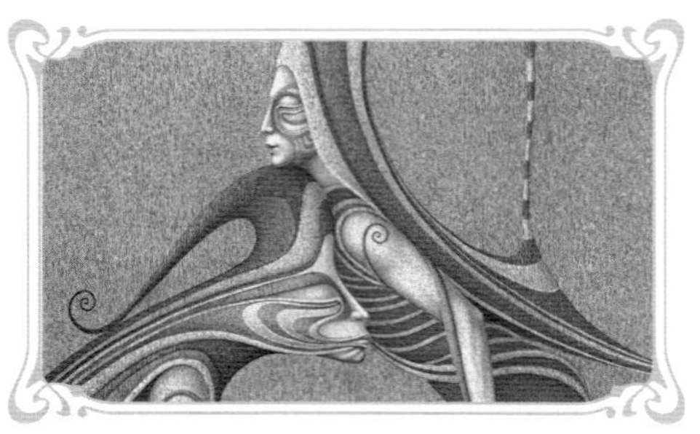

19
LOVE TO INTERACT

WATER • FEELINGS • EMOTIONS

Show your feelings.

Virtue is more to man than either water or fire. I have seen men die from treading on water and fire, but I have never seen a man die from treading the course of virtue.

— CONFUCIUS —

20
LOVE TO INTERACT
EARTH • MATERIAL WORLD

Take time to share your gifts.

One word frees us of all the weight and pain of life: that word is love.

— SOPHOCLES —

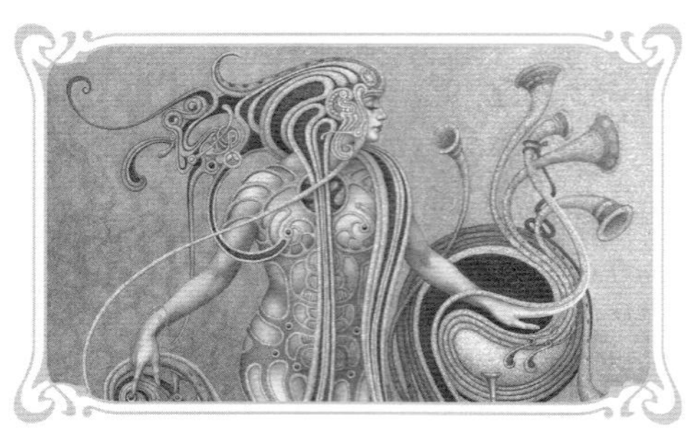

21
CONCEIVE, CREATE, IMPLEMENT

AIR • EXTERNAL EVENTS

New creative opportunities come up. You will meet like-minded people.

Opportunities don't happen, you create them.

— CHRIS GROSSER —

22
CONCEIVE, CREATE, IMPLEMENT

FIRE • ACTION

Let your creative potential take control.

Always dream and shoot higher than you know you can do. Do not bother just to be better than your contemporaries or predecessors. Try to be better than yourself.

— WILLIAM FAULKNER —

23
CONCEIVE, CREATE, IMPLEMENT

WATER • FEELINGS • EMOTIONS

Don't be afraid to be funny.
Give way to your emotions.
It's time to be yourself.

Your time is limited, so don't waste it living someone else's life.

— STEVE JOBS —

24
CONCEIVE, CREATE, IMPLEMENT
EARTH • MATERIAL WORLD

Start a new project.
Follow your dream.

Live as if you were to die tomorrow.
Learn as if you were to live forever.

— MAHATMA GANDHI —

25
PERCEIVE, LEARN, BE AWARE

AIR • EXTERNAL EVENTS

Change of perception,
examine your worldview.

The mind is everything.
What you think you become.

— BUDDHA —

26
PERCEIVE, LEARN, BE AWARE

FIRE • ACTION

Get ready to be influenced by a strong individual. Start learning.

Learning is a treasure that will follow its owner everywhere.

(CHINESE PROVERB)

27
PERCEIVE, LEARN, BE AWARE

WATER • FEELINGS • EMOTIONS

Be open to new impressions and interesting information.

*We do not remember days,
we remember moments.*

— CESARE PAVESE —

28
PERCEIVE, LEARN, BE AWARE

EARTH • MATERIAL WORLD

Engage with interesting people, stimulating travel and unexpected discoveries.

Love all, trust a few,
do wrong to none.

— WILLIAM SHAKESPEARE —

29
MAKE A CHANGE, TRANSFORM

AIR • EXTERNAL EVENTS

Expect a miracle;
it's always nearby.

While I'm breathing, I love and believe.

30
MAKE A CHANGE, TRANSFORM

FIRE • ACTION

Time to change.
Throw away everything old
and start over.

Start where you are. Use what you have. Do what you can.

— ARTHUR ASHE —

31
MAKE A CHANGE, TRANSFORM

WATER • FEELINGS • EMOTIONS

Feel energized.
Anything is possible.

I am not a product of my circumstances.
I am a product of my decisions.

— STEPHEN COVEY —

32
MAKE A CHANGE, TRANSFORM

EARTH • MATERIAL WORLD

Don't be afraid of change.
Make the first step.

Life is not about waiting for the storm to pass; it's about learning to dance in the rain.

— VIVIAN GREENE —

33

DREAM

AIR • EXTERNAL EVENTS

Soon you will find out
that dreams do come true.

*Miracles happen to those
who believe in them.*

— BERNARD BERENSON —

34
DREAM
FIRE • ACTION

Soldier on.
Luck is on your side.

Either write something worth reading
or do something worth writing.

— BENJAMIN FRANKLIN —

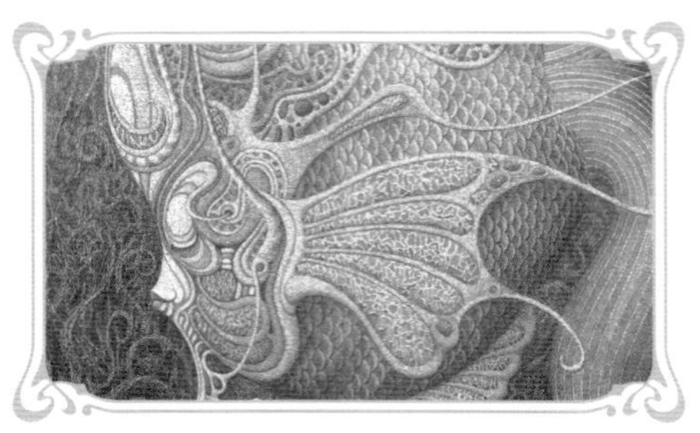

35
DREAM
WATER • FEELINGS • EMOTIONS

Good things will come
when you stay positive.

You are the creator of your own destiny.

— SWAMI VIVEKANANDA —

36
DREAM
EARTH • MATERIAL WORLD

Talk about your dreams.

The past cannot be changed.
The future is yet in your power.

— MARY PICKFORD —

37
GROW AND LEARN

AIR • EXTERNAL EVENTS

A new purpose will enrich your inner potential and help your transformation.

In the middle of difficulty
lies opportunity.

— ALBERT EINSTEIN —

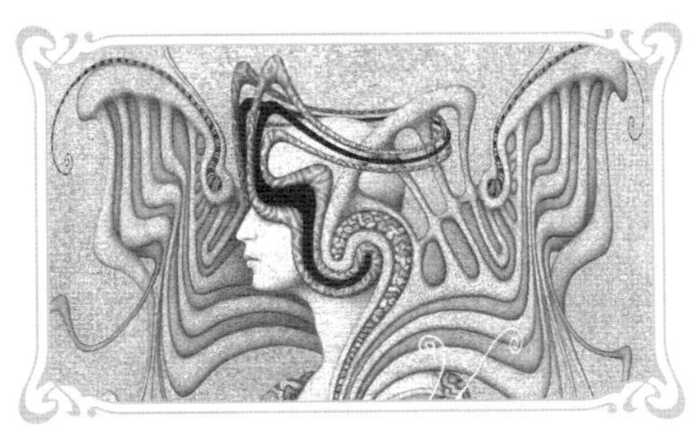

38
GROW AND LEARN
FIRE • MATERIAL WORLD

Stop your stream of thoughts.
Listen to the inner silence.

The foolish man seeks happiness in the distance; the wise grows it under his feet.

— JAMES OPPENHEIM —

39
GROW AND LEARN

WATER • FEELINGS • EMOTIONS

Be content with what you have.
Concentrate on something
you love to do.

*Build your own dreams, or someone
else will hire you to build theirs.*

— FARRAH GRAY —

40
GROW AND LEARN
EARTH • MATERIAL WORLD

Evolve.
Learn something new.
Take a master class.

Have no fear of perfection;
you'll never reach it.
— SALVADOR DALI —

41
DO WHAT YOU MUST AND COME WHAT MAY

ABOUT THE ARTIST

For Boris Indrikov, being creative means always wondering who he is. Born in Leningrad in 1967, Boris was introduced to art at a very young age. At first, he was oriented towards engineering and studied at the National University of Science and Technology (MISiS). Simultaneously, he designed books and started to work as an illustrator for the popular science magazine *Chemistry and Life*. He left the university in 1990, after realizing that art is what he really wanted to do. For Boris, working on a painting is like meditation and a kind of ritual.

> *An artist is a Creator of the parallel Universes. A language of art is the language in which we talk to God.*
>
> — BORIS INDRIKOV —

His passion for what he does enables Indrikov to create art pieces that have captivated many art lovers and followers. Boris has been a member of the Creative Union of Artists of Russia and the UNESCO International Federation of Artists since 1998. His work is influenced by Renaissance paintings, Art Nouveau, Asian art, contemporary science fiction and fantasy, all beautifully interlaced into his exceptional style.

Indrikov portrays mainly fantastic realism in his work. He creates a primarily realistic view of the real world but at the same time his art is filled with futuristic and imaginary elements. His works are exhibited in galleries and private collections in Russia, Italy, Germany, France, Japan and the United States.

I attended art courses at different studios taught by professional artists. But my main teachers are the masters of the European Renaissance, 14th–15th centuries.

— BORIS INDRIKOV —

Currently, Boris' studio is based in Moscow where he continues to work in painting. His collection includes numerous oil paintings, graphic design, and recently sculpture and fabric design.

To see his work, visit: www.indrikov.com

For our complete line of tarot decks, books, meditation cards, oracle sets, and other inspirational products please visit our website: www.usgamesinc.com

U.S. GAMES SYSTEMS, INC.
179 Ludlow Street
Stamford, CT 06902 USA
Phone: 203-353-8400
Order Desk: 800-544-2637
FAX: 203-353-8431